The Sin of Eli

Codependency and Enabling through the Biblical Lens

Erika Grey

Pedante Press

Advice for Life in These End Times Series

All Scriptural quotations in this publication are from the New King James Version of the Bible © by Thomas Nelson, Inc.

Printed in the United States of America

Copyright © 2021 Erika Grey

All rights reserved.

ISBN: 978-1-940844-28-2

DEDICATION

To my dear friend now caught up in this sin, may the Lord Jesus Christ help you break the chains of codependency and enabling and claim the victory that is yours in Him.

CONTENTS

	Acknowledgments	i
1	My Experience with Codependent Enablers	1
2	What is an Enabler?	5
3	Enabling is a Sin	15
4	Eli's Parenting	20
5	Eli's Sons of Belial	25
6	Blinders	30
7	Boundaries	39
8	Elis Son's Sins Are Also His	45
9	Victory Over Enabling	50
10	Judgement on Eli's Home	60

www.erikagrey.com

For Bible Prophecy news and analysis and more books visit my website. For Bible Prophecy Updates on video subscribe to my YouTube channel Prophecy Talk with Erika Grey.

1 MY EXPERIENCE WITH CODEPENDANT ENABLERS

I grew up with a mother who was one of the enabler varieties. I married another, who was not only the same brand as my mom, but whose own parent was of another type and enabled him when he relapsed into alcohol addiction. As someone who herself struggled with addictions, this world was all too familiar to me. One of my books deals with the topic. So, this is an area I have experience.

I recounted in my book "Free from Captivity: Biblical Secrets to Overcoming Addiction." the death of my husband from alcohol and heroin. As time went on it became apparent that he was given the heroin by his own brother and his friend to quiet him because he became loud and obnoxious. Three months later his brother died the same death.

Watching Sin Takeover My Friend

More recently my close friend in the Lord descended into the sin of enabling. Of all the ones I encountered, she surprised me the most. I had viewed her as such a strong individual. She was a prayer warrior, a woman who I admired for her spiritual strength. Yet she descended into the grievous sin of enabling her drug addicted relatives.

I watched as this God-fearing woman changed from a solid Christian to just as bad as the addicts she enabled, at which point I had to distance from the friendship we once shared. Despite my sound advice she chose her sin. As I would advise her in the situation, she lied to me and this is typical of a codependent or an enabler, they are both essentially one in the same.

Those Who Willfully Sin

The Scripture advises to break fellowship with a brother or sister in Christ who is willfully in sin. In that she was facilitating heroin addicts I told her that she might as well be doing the drug herself. No doubt heroin abuse is a dark sin. As typical of an enabler, my comments were met with denial and her belief that her relatives had stopped using drugs. As this book goes on it will reveal the facilitator's real deep-seated issues, which are the reason for these actions. As we look at Eli and the sin of enabling, we will examine codependency from the Biblical lens. You will learn the reason for the symbiotic relationship of the codependent enabler and the addict.

My Own Children's Recovery

The advice I gave my friend which she ignored had worked for my own children. An active alcoholic/addict reaps havoc in the family. Both of our children initially followed their father's path. But, I would not enable them. Moreover, God and the Lord Jesus Christ is first in my life. I determined as Joshua that me and my home would serve the Lord. Both of my kids are free from substance for some time now. It does not mean there are not other issues because in a family you will always deal with those, but there was victory and an end to the nightmare of their substance abuse.

The Story of Eli

At one point in my Biblical studies, I came across the story of Eli the priest and Judge of Israel. The Bible makes it clear that his sin was the sin of enabling. Eli enabled his wicked sons. His story provides a lot of insight that is revealed in this book. Thus, given my personal experience, I write this from both a Biblical perspective, experience, and my own observations. My hope is that if you are caught up in this sin that this book will give you insight from the Biblical perspective and help you to overcome this immorality and have the healing for you and your family members.

2 WHAT IS AN ENABLER

The definition of an enabler is a person or thing that makes something possible. More specifically a person who encourages or enables negative or self-destructive behavior in another. Being an enabler is a modern-day term that that goes along with today's social ills, especially in the world of addiction.

This is the area that enablers are the most destructive is in the lives of the addict. The addict is addicted to substance or other self-destructive behavior while the enabler is addicted to the addict. They bounce off each other and continue in both of their self-destructive behaviors. They are linked together like in a chain. The addict is an obvious menace, while the enabler appears to be the upstanding person. They are no different than the addict in their level of sin. They usually appear as good, and often do not partake in the substances or actions of their addict counterpart. In addition, there are also addicts who are enablers too.

Codependent

Enablers are also codependent. This is described as a person with an excessive emotional or psychological reliance on a partner. Typically, it is one who requires support on account of an illness or addiction. This reliance can extend to other relatives such as their children or parents. As was stated on the web they are addicted to the approval of people who are addicted to the power of withholding it.

Enablers Act Like Addicts

Enablers act like an addict in that they lie, make excuses for them, and totally make possible all the evil that the addict commits under the guise of loving them. But it is not love for the person at all. Not a Godly healthy love. Enablers just like addicts break up family's and relationships. I know of one man who is now divorced because his wife enabled a daughter and her worthless soon to be son in law who would not work or better himself. She even paid their rent and lied to her husband about it.

Enablers Actions Mask as Love

While enablers can also be addicts, there are those who do not touch substance at all. Many are upstanding citizens who state their love for the addict. In fact, their actions masquerade as love. The truth is that it is not love at all and reveals instead mental instability. Enablers become deceived into thinking they are doing what is best and are caring for their addicted loved ones when they are not caring at all. A person who enables has serious issues themselves. Enabling does not evidence love but rather neediness.

Enablers are Needy People.

An enabler desires the undivided attention from the addict they assist. They need that individual putting them on a pedestal. For this purpose, they establish themselves as the protector and rescuer in the person's life. They hope that those they enable will be indebted and tend to their needs. These includes giving the enabler their physical and emotional support.

Need to be liked, accepted.

The enabler has a great need to be liked and accepted. This is so great they deliberately aid and allow bad behavior to continue. For this reason, they fear setting boundaries. They exist in a symbiotic, codependent relationship with those they enable and feel liked as their help is accepted.

Low self esteem

Enablers have extremely low self-esteem. As a result, they have no sense of self and look to those they enable to provide this for them. A person with healthy self-esteem will set boundaries and have expectations. They are also not afraid to dish out consequences.

Lonely

Enablers are lonely and have a need to keep people close to them. They do not suffer the usual loneliness but rather theirs is joined with a deep void and feelings of emptiness. This traces back to their own trauma. The drama and turmoil from dealing with their addicts, or whatever bad behavior they help to continue, helps to fill this void. Addicts also suffer from this inner void. While the addict seeks substance to fill it, the enabler seeks the addict to satiate theirs.

Fear rejection

Enablers fear rejection. This fear is so great, that they look to gratify the needs of their addicted loved ones so that they will not be rejected by them. They look at a boundary as abandonment of the person they are enabling. Their own fear of rejection is so great that they distort boundaries as a means for the addict to abandon them.

Manipulative

By providing money, food, shelter, bond etc., enablers manipulate their family members into getting what they want. What they want the most is to be liked, accepted, and put on a pedestal by those they enable. After all, in their minds they are their rescuer. In addition, they want to exhibit control over the addict by their indebtedness. Even more so without knowing it they prey on the addicted to have a hold. More on this later.

Projection

According to psychiatry today, projection is the process of displacing one's feelings onto a different person, animal or object…Unconscious discomfort can lead people to attribute unacceptable feelings or impulses to someone else to avoid confronting them. Projection allows the difficult trait to be addressed without the individual fully recognizing it in themselves.

Enablers Project Themselves on Those They Aid

The enabler is not able to view those they are helping through a healthy lens. They see themselves and are essentially rescuing their inner self from their own trauma. They become hypersensitive of the afflictions of those they enable. They view any boundary or normal parenting action as a road to their being rejected, which they fear. They masquerade this for love and kindness. They are protecting themselves from rejection by those they facilitate. The sad reality is that in projecting they fail to see the truth of their situation.

Enablers are Rescuing Themselves.

While enabling is written about as mis guided caring for the enabled, it really is self-serving and does not care about the person at all. The enabler feeds off the weakness of the person they enable. They pit one parent against the other where they emerge as the understanding and helpful one.

The real god here is the god of being liked and their need to draw their children close to them and they act as the child's rescuer. Only an enabler does not save the child at all, instead their actions further lead the child down a self-destructive path. The enabler is rescuing themselves.

My Recent Discussion

Coincidentally I heard from my friend while writing this book. She phoned me because she had not heard from me in a while. She had helped get her niece a job caring for an elderly woman. She could not see anything wrong that she is driving this 28-year-old girl back and forth daily to this job. A girl who has been unable to get a job during her entire 20's, who this woman has gotten her all of her work. She supposedly has looked time and time again. When I asked if her 32-year-old nephew had gotten a vehicle yet, she said no, when I commented it has now been two years, she insisted it had not been that long. In fact, it has been longer, I commented that if he had not gotten one by now, he will not get one. No doubt she is still driving him and happily so. She is addicted to their need of her.

My Corrected Lens

As I stated I had always seen my friend as a strong Christian woman. Not only was she a prayer warrior but she is a Dorcas. This is the woman in the Bible who had a ministry making clothes for widows. She died and all the widows were crying. Peter raised her back to life from the dead (Acts 9:39-42).

My friend is willing to help any woman in need. Yet she was born with a noticeable disability. I thought she had overcome it in the Lord. Instead, I saw that it led her instead to choose sin. To my shock after a couple of conversations I realized she had self-hate over her disability. In addition to shame.

Shame

I wrote about the Bible's recognition of emotional shame in my book, "In Their Pain, Great Women of the Bible." It is associated with loss and trauma. Many feel there is something wrong with them when they are singled out for tragedy.

Disability falls under the scope of a tragedy. The enabler is governed by shame. The feeling that they are defective, unacceptable, and damaged beyond repair. As we will look at later, it is likely that Eli lost his wife and became a widower. So, he too ranked among those that suffered loss and tragedy.

Blindness and People Looking In

The enabler is blinded by their sin. People looking into the enabler's situation see the abnormality of it and see it clearly for what it is. Normal functioning households do not put up with bad, addictive, or delinquent behavior. They do not make excuses for it or protect it. They set expectations and have rules. Delinquent behavior and alcohol and drug use are dealt with appropriately. Boundaries are established. Bad behavior will bring consequences, while good behavior brings rewards. God Himself expects us to set boundaries in our households. In functioning homes there is order and structure. They are not hangouts of the able bodied who chose addiction and therefore do not work.

3 ENABLING IS A SIN

Enabling pure and simply is a sin. This is what we see in the Bible in the life of Eli. Eli was a priest who served in the Temple. He was the second to the last judge who ruled, followed by the prophet Samuel who anointed Saul as Israel's first King. Eli was a descendant of Moses. His son Gershom bore Shebuel, who was a ruler of the treasures (I Chronicles 26:24). He came to judge Israel at a time that Judges 21:25 wrote, *"In those days there was no king in Israel; everyone did what was right in his own eyes."*

Eli Served God and His Sons

Eli' major sin in his life, was that he was an

enabler of his son's evil deeds. Along with Eli we read the account of Hannah who was childless went to the Temple and prayed for a child. She cried in the anguish of her soul. Eli watched her lips move and accused her of being drunk. She told him that she did not drink at all but was pouring out her soul in her grief. He told her to *"Go in peace, and the God of Israel grant your petition which you have asked of Him."* Hannah was barren and she prayed for a child and God gave her a son. She brought the son to Eli to raise in the Temple as a priest because she had made this promise to God.

While Eli was enabling his sons, he was also serving God. This is like many enablers who lead a respected life compared to those they support in their sin. In addition to those that are born again Bible believing Christians. In the account we see Hannah's prayers answered. Samuel the prophet is even trained under the tutelage of Eli.

Eli's Sin Caused God's Blessing of His Word to Be Removed

Despite Eli's sin, Hannah has a miracle given to her by God and Samuel trains and grows in the Lord to the time of his calling. The passage tells us that *"And the word of the Lord was rate in those days; there was no widespread revelation.* Eli's sin of enabling his sons and their wicked deeds hindered God's Word from going forward. Yet we see Him work in the lives of those who sought him such as Hannah and her son Samuel. The land is what Eli reigned over, much like we over our households. So essentially the blessing was gone because of Eli's sin.

Enabler Lose God's Blessing

If you are enabling, you will lose God's blessing in your home. When you are dealing with addicted persons, these are the giants in the land that the books of Moses, Judges and Joshua with God's power defeat. We see that the sin of Achan kept Joshua from winning over a weaker enemy. The sin of enabling not only is a sin on the part of the person who enables, but also on those they facilitate in their transgressions. Therefore, God cannot work. In addition, as we will see from the story this sin brings consequences.

God Calls Samuel

When Eli was old God called Samuel. He

called his name and Samuel ran to Eli thinking that Eli had called him. After three times Samuel went to Eli thinking he called him. The Bible records in 1 Samuel 3: 8-10:

⁸And the LORD called Samuel again the third time. So, he arose and went to Eli, and said, "Here I am, for you did call me."

Then Eli perceived that the LORD had called the boy. ⁹Therefore Eli said to Samuel, "Go, lie down; and it shall be, if He calls you, that you must say, 'Speak, LORD, for Your servant hears.' " So Samuel went and lay down in his place.

¹⁰Now the LORD came and stood and called as at other times, "Samuel! Samuel!"

And Samuel answered, "Speak, for Your servant hears."

Eli Judged for His Sin of Placing His Sons Before God.

The first words of prophecy God speaks to Samuel are about how He is going to judge the house of Eli, *"for the iniquity which he knows, because his sons made themselves vile, and he did not restrain them.* In 1 Samuel 2: adds *"and honor your sons more than you honor me."*

The key is that his sin is putting those he enabled, which were his sons before God. This disobeys the first command to have no other gods before God. We know from Scripture that when someone makes something or someone a god, there come plagues. Plagues come with the idols. The enabler is always plagued with the behavior of those they enable, yet they do not stop enabling the behavior.
Through the enabler's neediness and lack of self-esteem Satan tempts the enabler to honor or love their relatives above god.

The Word used for Honor.

The word in the Hebrew for honor means, to cause to be honored: to glorify, to make glorious, promote. An enabler certainly puts the person before God and His commands. This is obvious in the life of Eli and his sons.

4 ELI'S PARENTING

Eli's parenting style was like the enablers close to me who suffered abuse as a child. They overcompensate for the strict, harsh, restrictive childhood they suffered through by having no boundaries for their own children.

My Mother's Story

My mother had been forced to carry cinder blocks as a young child. She remembers working and not being allowed to play. Her father was violent and abusive. He beat his wife and children. He tied my uncle to a bed. She recalled her father sticking his finger down one of their throats for so much as crying. My mother's parenting style became one of enabling. She did all the chores for her children. In addition, she set down no rules. She married my father who was a controlling man. He was harsh and violent at times. She established herself as both the victim of my father's harshness and our rescuer. She was our deliverer from his boundaries, the person we could go to when my dad said no.

Mom a People Pleaser

My mother was a people pleaser. She lived for being liked. She even sacrificed her own children on its altar. When I was a young teenager our home became a hangout. It was also the place we could hold alcohol fueled parties. Both of my parents enabled our drinking. I remember the horror of the relatives who would come for a visit. They voiced their shock at what was going on in our home. My own aunt told me that my mother's problem was that she had to be liked. She was correct.

Mom an Enabler

When I became born again right before my 18th birthday, the church families became an example for me. While I led my mother to the

Lord and she and my father both got saved, it took me a long time, hard knocks and God working in me to undo the damage that had been done. As I write this, now I understand her issues and parenting style which was the same as Eli's.

My Late Husband's story

On the other hand, my late husband was also a parent with an enabling style. He was abused by his mother. She whipped him with electrical cords. In addition, he was beaten almost nightly by his father as prompted by his mother. When our son was born, he would not let anyone near him, let alone create any kind of boundary or rule. When I created a chore for him, his would perform it on behalf of our son. Later when he became disabled and got addicted to pills and later drinking, his mother and sister enabled his substance abuse. If it were not for them, he might still be alive today.

Meanwhile when our son drank, his father enabled his drinking. Both my son and his dad ended up at my late husband's enabling mother's house. In understanding Eli and the Biblical account, I know that this originated from his pain and shame. My late husband just like my mother assumed the role of rescuer for their children. I am sure this was also Eli's role, that of the rescuer. But Eli along with my mother and late husband were also overcompensating.

Overcompensating

This parenting style on the part of abused, or traumatized individuals is one of overcompensating. They felt so abused and restricted as children that they do not give theirs any boundaries. They take care of all their unpleasant tasks for them.

Again, this is to win the child and begin a codependent relationship with them. This was the sin of Eli, he let his sons do as they wish. It was also characteristic of my enabling mother and late husband.

Eli Most Likely Lost His Wife.

In the Biblical account of Eli there is no mention of his wife. Even when judgement is pronounced on him and his sons, we have no details about her. This most likely indicates that Eli was a widower. His wife could have died in childbirth or from illness. He might have been codependent on his wife and from the time of her death his codependency transferred to his sons. After experiencing the loss of his wife, raising his boys without their mother could have caused Eli to overcompensate by allowing them to do what they wanted with no boundaries. His codependency and enabling would never have been an issue if God had been first in his life over his family.

5 ELI'S SONS OF BELIAL

The Bible states in 1 Samuel 1:16, *"Now the sons of Eli were sons of Belial, they knew not the LORD."* This is obvious by their actions. They committed grievous sins within the temple. These included bullying those giving the offerings and taking portions before they were sacrificed to God. In addition, they collected more meat than allowed by the law. If this was not bad enough, they were having sexual relations with women of the Tabernacle, who assembled at the Tent of Meeting. One writer indicated these women could have been raped.

Belial-Evil Worthless

The word belial is used 17 times in 16 verses

in the Bible. Belial in the Hebrew means worthless, good for nothing, unprofitable, or without profit, base fellow, wicked, ruin and destruction. In addition, belial means wickedness, evil, naughty, ungodly (men) who are wicked. Other words used are vileness, an evil wicked thing, a wicked woman, and a destroyer. While this sounds repetitive it adds, unprofitable, worthlessness, what is useless, of no fruit, of no profit, of little worth.

Not my Son or Daughter

Before I go further with the definition, enablers reading this will not think that their evil little angels fit this description. I can still hear my diseased mother-in-law saying how good her son was who used heroin. How he was such a hard worker. Meanwhile he abandoned his family for drugs. In addition, he paid no support for his children. Moreover, he swindled his former wife every way he could and lied to his mother continuously to get money from her for drugs. This is the song of every enabler concerning those they enable.

Children of Belial are Idolators.

In the Old Testament the word is used

referring to idolatry, *"the children of Belial who enticed others to go and serve other gods, "which ye have not known"* (Deuteronomy 13:13). If they are abusing drugs or alcohol the substance is the idol. 2 Timothy 3:1-5 states that men will be lovers of pleasure more than lovers of God. When one partakes in alcohol or drug addiction, they are seeking the god of pleasure.

Violent and Sexually Immoral-Perverted

In Judges 19:22 sons of Belial knock on the door of a man's house to pull out a fellow that visited him so that they can rape him. Some verses call them perverted men. Instead, they took the man's concubine, abused her all night which led to her dying as she reached her husband's home.

Drunkards, Rebels, Murderers, Violent and Liars

When Eli accused Hannah of being drunk while she was praying, she stated, *"Count not thine handmaid for a daughter of Belial: for out of the abundance of my complaint and grief have I spoken hitherto."* (1 Samuel 1:16). This makes it clear that a drunkard is a child of Belial. We can extend this to any kind of drug addict or substance abuser as well.

In 1 Samuel 10: 27, and 2 Samuel 20: 1, we see the children of Belial referred to as rebels, who refuse to do the will of God and do not honor the king that God established in Israel. The verse records that they "despised him." In 1 Samuel 30:22 they are associated with wicked men. In addition, with bloodthirsty men or murders (2 Samuel 16:7).

In 1 Kings 21:13 we see they are liars and were responsible for the death of Naboth by Ahaz and Jezebel. Therefore, they are liars and violent. In 2 Chronicles 13:7, we see them fighting against Rehoboam who was described as young and tenderhearted, and he could not withstand them.

Equivalent with Satan

Finally, in 2 Corinthians 6:15, the definition in the Greek is "the worthless or wicked" and Belial is a name of Satan. In this verse Paul clearly states, *"And what accord has Christ with Belial? Or what part has a believer with an unbeliever?*

In addition to Eli's sons associated with Belial, each of their names bears negative significance. Hopni in Hebrew defines as a pugilist or fighter. This is not in a good sense as he acted like a bully. Phinehas in the Hebrew means "mouth of brass' and is a variation of mouth of a serpent. A serpent in the Bible represents Satan.

Godless

We can see that sons of Belial fit all drug addicts, alcoholics, rebels, and criminals. The Bible makes it clear that these do not know God. If they knew the Lord, they would not be living their evil lifestyle. It needs to be noted that Eli's sons worked as priests in the temple. They most likely knew the religious phrases. Both of Eli's sons could speak them when it suited their purposes, but they were Godless. The other message here is that Eli's enabling parenting style contributed to his son's delinquency. In addition to their Godlessness.

6 BLINDERS

Enablers have blinders over their eyes when it comes to the evil behavior of their loved ones. This is because the sin of addiction blinds. The enabler is addicted to the addict in their lives. In the story of Sampson who was a love addict, when he gives his heart to Delilah, he ends up in the prison house and is blinded. Sampson's story is a clear picture of what happens in addiction. This also happens to the facilitators of the sons and daughters of Belial.

They Only See Them as Good

My late husband who guarded our son from birth and kept him from doing chores would tell everyone what a good kid he was while he was acting like a total brat. My former friend who is enabling junkies at her home and housing them will tell you what hard workers they are, how good they are despite their lying to her continuously and having most likely turned her home into their shooting gallery and crack smoking den.

She makes excuses on how they cannot get work. In addition to why they do not have money and why they cannot get a car on the road. One time when I pointed out how many years, they lived with her she even minimized the number of years by about three. She takes them to get their methadone even though I told her that junkies stay on methadone to sell it for heroin and to keep their addictions at bay.

I think of my mother-in-law talking about how good her son was. This was after he became a junkie, abandoned his family, and was lying and conning her to get money. In addition to his beating the system in any way possible to continue shooting dope.

An extreme is Chris Watt's mother. He is the psychopath who murdered his entire family. This included his beautiful wife Shannan and their two daughters Bella and

CeCe. His mother blamed Shannan for the death of the two precious little girls. We also see this in Eli. While the Bible does not say specifically, the fact that Eli allowed his sons to serve in the Temple signifies that he did not see them for what they had become.

Total Blindness

The total blindness that takes over an enabler is mind staggering. Despite the family members going to my mother-in-law and telling her about her one son's heroin use and taking her money for heroin, she still believed his lies. He even got to the point of demanding the money from her. He had so many DUI's that he permanently lost his driver's license. He even went to jail. Despite the needles around the home, and his behavior, she still gave him money and talked highly of him.

Concerning my late husband, his drunkenness upset her household. One day when I went to get him help to get clean, as he was falling drunk walking with me holding him, his mother angrily asked where I was taking him. When I told her, she tried to tell me he was fine. She did not want him to leave and was blinded to the spectacle he had become.

The same happened with my friend. I relayed to her the articles of her nephew getting arrested for shooting heroin in a store parking lot. Moreover, I provided her the real facts of a lie he told her, that another of his arrests was over crack cocaine. In addition, I gave her much more information, it did not matter. Her addiction to them and need of them overtook all reasoning and logic and completely blinded her.

Who knows how far this had actually gone, maybe even to the point of her buying them drugs. This would not surprise me as I had been on the phone and overheard her niece demanding money. This friend of mine would not want her niece to suffer withdrawal pain. She might even be doing drugs herself to join them.

Using Drugs with Them

I knew of a Christian woman who had a previous drug problem. Her daughter started using crack cocaine, which she stood against. One day she sat down and took a hit off a crack pipe to see what her daughter was doing and why she was using this drug. She smoked it with her. Her son also has serious addiction issues with marijuana, and now Adderall. It should go without saying that there is no victory in their family.

I remember the time a party was going on at my home before I got saved. My dad stated that he wanted to try weed to see why we were using it. Nothing endorsed my alcohol and drug use than by him not only allowing our parties, but then offering to smoke weed with us.

My former husband shocked my sons and his friends on the way to a ski trip in Vermont. He pulled out a joint and started to smoke it and shared it with them. I did not learn of this until after he was deceased. He hid from me as much as he was possibly able. After he entered the drug world of crack cocaine, I was horrified to learn of the fathers who smoked crack with their sons, and mothers with their daughters.

Not all enablers partake in the sins of their addicts. This was not characteristic of Eli. Never-the-less how could he have his sons serve in the Temple when they were committing such gross sins? He heard about their evil deeds. Like all enablers he refused to see or accept it until finally confronted by the prophet Samuel.

Projection and Shame

Earlier we talked about enabler projecting themselves onto their children. With all their other ill feelings about themselves they carry a lot of shame. They are almost incapable of admitting that anything is wrong with the family member they enable. It is part of their addiction to the person. With bondage comes denial. All active addicts live in a state of denial. Enabling is a form of addiction and they deny their addicts problem is as severe as it is to help eliminate their own shame.

When my friend's niece was sent to prison or jail for her charges, she lied to me and told me that she went to a rehab. While lying to me about the real whereabouts of her relative, she tried to tell me how her niece attended church there and was reading her Bible. I insisted that there are no churches in rehab. I know that from having been in one myself.

My friend was protecting her own shame by lying to protect her relative from anyone having any ill thoughts about her being in prison. Essentially the person they enable is a substitute for them. In addition, they lie to cover their sin and the extent to which they enable. Enablers lie the same way as drug addicts and alcoholics to hide their sin.

Need of the Person

Another reason for the blindness is their own need of their family member. They keep hoping and believing they are on the road to getting better. A day or two without a drink, a new job, their voicing future goals, all of this gives the enabler hope that the person will be there for them.

In Eli's case, after the probable death of his wife he was left alone. Instead of seeking God who he served to meet his needs he looked to his sons. The sad reality is that the enabler needs the person they enable more than they are in want of them.

To onlookers it does not appear that way because addicts are without housing and vehicles. The enabler has these things. But once the addict cleans up they will no longer have need of the enabler, while it is not true in the reverse. Deep down an enabler does not want the person to get better because that will mean that they will no longer require their help.

Fear

Enabling is done out of fear. In the case of my friend, she allowed the man who started her niece on heroin to live in the home. She felt it kept her niece in her sight. She had so much anxiety each time her niece went out that she permitted a man to live there who should have been forbidden in her house.

My own father allowed us kids to drink in the home with the thought that he would rather it be in front of him than out of the house. Meanwhile we were able to have parties and black out at them right in our own home. This kept us drinking with no consequences to motivate us to stop.

Rationalization

Along with fear some rationalize that if they do not enable the situation could be worse and their loved one could end up on the streets or in jail. There is no doubt there is a serious level of danger out there especially if the addicts are young women, and you need wisdom, but many of the above fears are irrational and illogical and keeps the enabler enabling.

Enabling Masquerades as Love

The final area of blindness on the part of the enabler is that they love their relatives. The only person an enabler love is themselves. As Eli honored his sons before God, he was really looking out for himself and not what was in their best interest. When you really love someone, you do not want them harming themselves. You want them to be functioning members of society. You will never want anyone you love destroying themselves with an alcohol or a drug addiction.

7 BOUNDARIES

Joshua 24:15 states, *"As for me and my house we will serve the Lord."* When one makes this commitment, they are essentially establishing boundaries within their home. The one thing that the enabler will not do is set up any boundaries. In part because people like their sin. An enabler is addicted to the addict. Just as the addict does not want to give up substance, the enabler does not want to give up the addict. Or the person whose bad behavior they enable.

Rules and Expectations

Boundaries in a home are a set of rules and expectations. When we put God first, we establish his boundaries in our home. Such as separating from the world, not allowing sinful items and symbols, and we reward good behavior and have consequences for evil actions. In addition, we strive to put God first and love Him and our neighbors. Rules and expectations are especially important when dealing with emotionally damaged individuals. Lights out time, no alcohol or drugs in the home, or drug and alcohol addicted friends. These are some examples. Church attendance is another.

Structure

Enabler's homes lack any kind of order. There are no rules or expectations and therefor no structure in the home. Anyone with any kind of mental health issues, such as addiction or those that lead to delinquent behavior need to be in an environment where they know what to expect. They need boundaries, to know those areas that if they venture into, they will suffer consequences. As much as they fight to control in their home, they are out of control when they rule it. Enablers give those they enable the control. They have a hold on the enabler because the enabler needs them for their self-worth and more.

In my friend's home her young adults are up at all hours of the night disturbing her sleep. She lets it continue for fear that a rule such as a lights out time will push them away. She also fears the threats of suicide from her niece. In addition to fears of her getting abducted. I warned my friend that her niece might already be turning tricks as a prostitute to fund her drug habit. The reality is that the greatest risk, that of an overdose will most likely happen in her own home.

In the case of Eli, it is obvious he had no structure, rules or expectations for his sons, and they were controlling the goings on in the Temple.

The Absurdity

The lack of structure in the home of an enabler becomes absurd. This defines as wildly unreasonable, illogical, or inappropriate. I think of the time when I was 14 and my brother was getting married. Instead of a wedding in a hall, my parents threw a large party at our home. The youth and young adults ended up in my room. There was literally wall to wall drinks on my bedroom furniture. I was nearly passed out on my bed. I had a black light and one of the young women was an artist. She painted obscenities on another young man dancing under the black light in florescent paint. She even painted his tongue. He took his clothes off and was dancing.

A young cousin came upstairs and ran back down to the adults and screamed, "they are taking their clothes off up there." I heard my aunts yelling to my mother that she better go upstairs and see what was going on. Meanwhile the young man's sister tells him he better get his pants on and he is extremely drunk. She helps him to get his pants on while my mother is marching up the stairs. As soon as my mother walked in the room, this man called my mother's name and dropped his pants and mooned her. My mother laughed and walked back down the stairs saying, "their just having fun."

Consequences

The Bible tells us that Eli did not restrain his sons and this means there were no boundaries or rules, expectations, or consequences for their actions. Part of having boundaries in your home is having consequences for when the rules are broken.

The Bible is clear that the Lord chastens us and we are to follow God's example. An example of this would mean not bailing their relative out of jail for drug use or stealing. The greatest weight held over their head is a place to live.

Time Frames

My friend drives her niece and nephew to the methadone clinic daily, she has been doing it for about a handful of years now. Despite my telling her that junkies sell the methadone for heroin, this did not phase her. I advised her to demand that they come off the methadone and give them a timetable. The consequence is they will not have a place to live. She instead described the pain and discomfort they experience during withdrawal and how they needed the methadone to prevent it. I told her of others who have gone cold turkey. In addition, I said to her, "too bad, that is the price they pay for getting on heroin.

Enabling Does Not Achieve What They Expect

Somehow, my friend expects that her relatives are going to want to stop doing drugs on their own. She also believes them when they lie to her. All she can see at her old age is that they need her and are keeping her from being alone. In addition, they will be there to care for her as she continues to age. She refuses to set any boundaries.

My now diseased mother-in-law enabled her two sons with the same fears. She passed away almost nine years after the death of her sons by overdoses. She was never the same after their death. Although she objected, her alcoholic daughter placed her in an assisted living facility. The last years of her life were ones of torment. She died the way she thought she was preventing by enabling- very much alone.

To make matters worse in the last four weeks of her life she fell off her wheelchair and broke her collar bone and three ribs. Her daughter a nurse by profession told the other nurses not to give her morphine. Her logic was that she wanted her to awake the times she might visit. She could not move without experiencing the sharp pain from her broken bones. During her final couple of days Hospice overruled her decision. Her mother was finally given morphine. It was a horrible end to the sad last decade of her life.

8 ELI'S SON'S SINS ALSO ARE HIS

In God's eyes, the enabler is as guilty as those they enable of the same sins. Enablers do not see it this way. They will tell you that they are against the behavior they enable. While they facilitate the bad actions, they hope that the person will realize what their lifestyle is doing to them and come to their senses. They do not comprehend that if they set boundaries, they can help this process along. In addition, by facilitating they are only adding to the problem behavior continuing.

Eli Did Not Set Boundaries.

In Samuel 2: 12-17 we see that Eli's sons Hophni and Phinehas went to those offering a sacrifice and demanded the meat for themselves. They even threatened to take it by force. The Bible says that people hated the sacrifice. Eli's sons bullied those who offered it. 1 Samuel 2: 22, adds that they were also having sexual relations with the women who gathered at the door of the tabernacle. In 1 Samuel 2:23 it tells us that when Eli heard what his sons did in all of Israel,

²³" So he said to them, "Why do you do such things? For I hear of your evil dealings from all the people. ²⁴ No, my sons! For it is not a good report that I hear. You make the LORD's people transgress. ²⁵ If one-man sins against another, God will judge him. But if a man sins against the LORD, who will intercede for him?"

Eli's Son's Did Not Listen to Him

The verse concludes saying that Eli's sons did not listen to him because the Lord had decided to kill them. Their sin was this great in Israel. Such is also the end of many drug addicts who die of overdoses. In addition to alcoholics who die of accidents or damage to their own liver. If Eli had established boundaries his sons would have listened to him, but there were no boundaries. This is evident by his saying that they should not do these things. Just like all enablers. If he meant it, he would have forbidden them from entering the temple and would have enforced this. From the time of their first misdeed would have been consequences.

Had Eli established boundaries they would have responded to his words. This should be a message to all enablers who think that as they enable their children will listen to them concerning their bad behavior.

By Their Fruits Ye Shall Know Them

Matthew 7:16-20 states, *"Ye shall know them by their fruits."* An addict also knows an enabler by their actions. They know that their words do not match their actions. There is no teeth to what they say. They know their enabler's fears and will use these to keep them in line. An example is threats of suicide or leaving them. The enabler and the addict are one, they do not function without each other.

My friend's niece would threaten suicide. My former husband would tell his mother she would never see him again. Both knew how to keep their enablers in line and get money from them. They also notice the enabler does not mean what they say. They know their fruits.

Two Sides of the Same Coin

The addict and the enabler are joined together but with two different functions in the committing of the same sin. They are two links in the same chain. While one commits the sin, the enabler makes it possible for the transgression to occur.

On some level the enabler wants the addict addicted because this keeps them dependent on them. An extreme picture of this is a pimp who deliberately gets his prostitute addicted to heroin to keep her in obedience and reliance and turning tricks for him. While the pimp is deliberate, the enabler might not even realize they are doing this. We view the pimp as evil and the prostitute a victim of the pimp. It is similar with an enabler to the addict they facilitate.

In God's Eyes

When God approaches Eli, he considers his son's sins, Eli's sins. 1 Samuel 2:27-29 affirms:

²⁷ Then a man of God came to Eli and said to him, "Thus says the LORD: 'Did I not clearly reveal Myself to the house of your father when they were in Egypt in Pharaoh's house? ²⁸ Did I not choose him out of all the tribes of Israel to be My priest, to offer upon My altar, to burn incense, and to wear an ephod before Me? And did I not give to the house of your father all the offerings of the children of Israel made by fire? ²⁹ Why do you kick at My sacrifice and My offering which I have commanded in My dwelling place, and honor your sons more than Me, to make yourselves fat with the best of all the offerings of Israel My people?'

In God's eyes if you make the ability for someone to sin such as use alcohol or drugs you are just as sinful as the person using the drugs.

In addition to equating Eli's sins as one with his sons for allowing them to continue in that behavior, God states that Eli is making himself fat with the best of Israel's offerings. In addition, that he is kicking at His sacrifice. Since Eli did not stop his sons he was as guilty as his sons and in a sense more guilty than them.

9 VICTORY OVER ENABLING

Enabling is a violation of the 1st Commandment: *"I am the Lord thy God, Thou shalt have no other gods before me."*

Jesus said in Matthew 10:37-39: *³⁷He who loves father or mother more than Me is not worthy of Me. And he who loves son or daughter more than Me is not worthy of Me. ³⁸And he who does not take his cross and follow after Me is not worthy of Me. ³⁹He who finds his life will lose it, and he who loses his life for My sake will find it.*

The enabler loves their family member more than God and more than Jesus. If the Lord were first, they would establish boundaries based on God's commands.

The Word Used for Love

The word used in the Greek for love in this verse is fileho. It is not the agapao love, which always references God's love toward us. Agapao defines as regarding the welfare of the person. Fileho on the other hand means, "to approve of, to like, to treat affectionately, or kindly, befriend and to delight in. Another words, it is a love that is self-serving and does not love as God loves.

From Experience

My son's drinking got out of control and his behavior became unpredictable. I threw him out of our home. In my home is a zero tolerance for alcohol or any of its symbols etc. One relative herself an enabler thought my actions were shocking.

I am happy to tell you that today my son has not had a drink for over eight years now. My daughter is also drug free. In addition, I have a cousin who is a solid Christian. She got saved later in life. Her son got addicted to heroin. She refused to enable him and implemented tough love. God is first in her life. Today he is clean for a good number of years now.

Sin in the Camp

A big lesson from the book of Joshua is that God does not provide victory when there is sin in the camp. Joshua 7 records the story of Achan's sin that kept Joshua from winning a victory against a small, weak enemy. We see that God work miracles of deliverance when He is put first. The closer we get to God the more we hate sin.

The Enablers Greatest Sin

The enabler's greatest sin is that they are not honoring God first, but rather themselves and those they enable. The real problem lies with the mental health of the enabler. Its more about their needs than those they facilitate. In the end they commit the same sin as those they help by allowing the bad behavior.

Fix the List

As an enabler you must take a good look at yourself and confess your sin of idolatry of honoring those you enable more than God. You must also look to God to heal your brokenness that led you to commit this sin to begin with.

Needy

Aa an enabler you must realize your neediness and not look for this child or adult's undivided attention. You must stop seeking to be put on a pedestal as rescuer. Realize that you are being motivated by your own neediness.

Stop the Role as Rescuer.

As an enabler you must step out of the role as the addict's rescuer. You assume this position because it makes you feel secure in the addict's life. Being their rescuer is delusional thinking. If anything, as an enabler you are their destroyer. Realize that you are not a rescuer and that your belief is a delusion. The addict will survive without you.

Need to be Liked, Accepted.

Realize as an enabler you have a need to be liked, so much so that you have let go of boundaries. You have sacrificed your addicted family member on the altar of you being liked. In addition, your need hurts others by enabling them. Just as the addict tramples on others to have his addiction, you damage the addict to be put on a pedestal by them.

Low Self Esteem

Understand that you have exceptionally low self-esteem. Yours is to the point of needing your validation from those you enable. Do not look to anyone to make you feel better about yourself. You do not have to do things for people or give them money to get them to like you. Look to God and His value on you. He says that we are a jewel in his crown.

Lonely

Admit that you are lonely and deal with your loneliness than by hurting addicted family members to keep them close to you. The desolation you feel is also an emptiness that originated with your trauma. Only Jesus can lift it. Look to Him to heal you.

Fear of Rejection

Deal with your fear of rejection. Do not worry if those you enable reject you by your setting boundaries. They will have more respect and love for you later. By giving into them you will bring the cold shoulder to pass if they get better from their addition.

Manipulative

Realize that you are manipulative and that you are not really loving those you enable. You are trying to keep them close to you. The money and provision you provide you use as a tool to lead them to believe you are helping them. If you put stipulations around the money and provisions, you would be using it as a constructive tool in their life.

Projection

Stop projecting your pain onto those you enable. Deal with your trauma. Do not limit their ability to move forward because you were not able to progress from yours. Stop projecting your pain onto them. Empathy does not excuse bad behavior.

Stop Irrational Fear

While a certain amount of fear is warranted, most are irrational. Examine its origins. Remember that when you take care of God's business in your life, He will take care of yours. Fear God first. The fear of the Lord is the beginning of wisdom. Satan uses the fear to keep you addicted to your addict.

Blindness-Open Your Eyes

Anyone who has established boundaries in their homes looks at yours and sees insanity. No one in their right mind facilitates family members who are drug addicts, active alcoholics, and junkies. No matter how you have lied to yourself to see your addicts as good people, God sees them as sons and daughters of Belial while they are serving Satan. If they are using drugs and alcohol, they are not serving God or living a righteous life.

If You Really Loved Them

Many addicts and delinquents suffer mental health issues. Those with them do best with structure and boundaries. If you really loved your family members you would do what was best for them. You would want them to be able to support themselves, to fend for themselves. In addition to becoming responsible citizens. You will train them for this. A mother bird trains its young chick to leave the nest and fly on its own. You are not loving your family members by keeping them attached to you. You are loving yourself first and foremost. You are hurting them and contributing to their destruction.

How Can an Enabler Get Victory?

Establish as Joshua that you will serve the Lord, you, and your house. God's rules will become yours in your home. Confess your sin and examine yourself. Make sure you put God first and be in obedience to His commands. Read your Bible. Have a zero tolerance for sin. Do not allow any symbols or people in the home associated with the addict's sin. Provide rules and timetables for your family members getting jobs, vehicles, paying rent, NA meetings, and church attendance, etc.

Say No

Learn to say no. To leave them in jail. To let them pay for their consequences. Do not bail them out. If they are on methadone give them a time frame to get off it. Do not believe their lies. Boundaries are what they need! The saddest part about the enabler not setting boundaries is that they are denying their family members what they need for their mental health. Most who get caught up in addiction suffer mental health issues. If you are parenting someone with mental health issues, they need structure and boundaries first and foremost.

Let Jesus Deliver You from Your Shame

Human Predators prey on the weak and vulnerable to commit their crime. As an enabler, you are a type of a predator who steps in as a rescuer to maintain a hold on the person's life. While you may state that you hate the bad behavior, you only want it gone in a way that allows you maintain your role as rescuer.

For the most part you help cover up the addict's sin, lie about it and deny it. You project your shame onto those in your grasp. Therefore, as an enabler you must deal with your shame or feeling that there is something wrong with you. Deliverance from your self-disgust is only through the Lord Jesus Christ. In addition, He gives us honor instead of shame.

Isaiah 61:7 promises double honor for shame:

Instead of your shame *you shall have* double *honor,*
And *instead of* confusion they shall rejoice in their portion.
Therefore in their land they shall possess double; Everlasting joy shall be theirs.

10 JUDGEMENT ON ELI'S HOME

Sin always brings consequences. Concerning idolatry, the Bible tells us that demons are in the idols. In addition, plagues come with idolatry. For the addict, this comes with their addiction and for the enabler, it comes by facilitating the addict and living with their toxic behavior and drama they bring into the household.

Consume Your Eyes and Grieve Your Heart

In Eli's case the sin was judged with death of the members of the entire household. Remember, their sin was committed in God's holy place: His *"dwelling place."* God said in 1 Samuel 2:30," *for those who honor Me I will honor, and those who despise Me shall be lightly esteemed."* God told Elithat He would cut off Eli's house meaning that he would have no living descendants. Those who God does not cut off will *"consume your eyes and grieve your heart. And all the descendants of your house shall die in the flower of their age."*

This is exactly what happens in the life of an enabler, the person they enable consumes them and grieves their heart as well, another words, breaks their heart. Even worse many addicts die in the flower of their age. Their sin causes them to die at a young age.

Eli's and His Son's Death

The Philistines went into battle against Israel and defeated the Israelites. They took the Ark of God and killed Eli's two sons. A man of the tribe of Benjamin left the army and went to Shiloh in great distress and told everyone in the city what happened. Eli heard the noise of the crying and asked, what was going on and why were people upset. The man came to him quickly. Eli was 97 years old and could not see well. According to 2 Samuel 1:4:16-18, which records the death of Eli *⁶Then the man said to Eli, "I am he who came from the battle. And I fled today from the battle line."*

And he said, "What happened, my son?"

¹⁷So the messenger answered and said, "Israel has fled before the Philistines, and there has been a great slaughter among the people. Also your two sons, Hophni and Phinehas, are dead; and the ark of God has been captured."

¹⁸Then it happened, when he made mention of the ark of God, that Eli fell off the seat backward by the side of the gate; and his neck was broken and he died, for the man was old and heavy. And he had judged Israel forty years.

Ichabod

Right after Eli and his son's deaths, his daughter in law, Phinehas's wife who was due to deliver their baby, on hearing the news of the deaths and the capture of the Ark of God, gave birth. While dying in childbirth and barely responding from the shock of the news she named the child Ichabod meaning, "The glory has departed from Israel."

Eli's story had a tragic ending. God's glory departed because of the level of sin in Eli's home. Both of his sons died. Eli on hearing the news of their deaths fell over and broke his neck because he was overweight.

Never a Happy Ending

Unfortunately, this happens in the homes of addicts, not just one death but two. Several of the situations I referenced in this book have not had joyful conclusions.

My own mother-in-law lost her two sons to drug overdoses three months apart. She said to me that she should have never provided her sons her house to live or given them both money. It was in fact money she gave them by listening to their lies that they bought the drugs that they overdosed on.

My former mother-in-law went onto live almost nine years past the date of their deaths and was never the same emotionally or mentally. She did not live, she existed in a hell of torment from the losses.

The woman who enabled her daughter to have a good for nothing boyfriend and paid their rent behind her husband's back ended in disaster as well. Not only is she divorced because her husband could not deal with her enabling, but the boy who she facilitated and helped pay the rent for, got a girlfriend, and divorced their daughter. He owes child support in addition to money to a former landlord who he stiffed for five months' rent.

I know another Christian woman, upstanding in her church who has two sons that are junkies, she has enabled them both. One died in a fiery car crash; it was his 14th car wreck. This killed him just after he got out of jail. The other is living at home still on methadone, and he continues to shoot dope.

Fine Lines and Grey Areas

There are always issues in life and parenting is hard. Sometimes there are fine lines and grey areas. In addition to tough decisions. Moreover, we all do not always get it right, even as we look to Jesus and the Bible as our guide. But, as we put God first, we can heal and our homes will follow, and we don't have to end up like Eli who was judged as harshly as his sons.

Your Choice

If you are an enabler and have read this book, the choice is yours. As you can see the ending for the enabler is not a good one, and neither for the addicts they facilitate. In Joshua 24:15, he stated, " *[15] And if it seems evil to you to serve the LORD, choose for yourselves this day whom you will serve, whether the gods which your fathers served that were on the other side of the River, or the gods of the Amorites, in whose land you dwell. But as for me and my house, we will serve the LORD."*

Genesis 4 tells the story of Cain and Abel's offering. Abel gave God his top- of- the- line, while Cain saved the best for himself and gave God the leftover. God accepted Abel's offering but did not respect Cains. This made Cain angry and jealous of Abel.

Genesis 4: 7 records that God said to Cain, *"And if you do well, will you not be accepted: And if you do not do well, sin lies at the door. And its desire is for you, but you should rule over it."*

As the story unfolded Cain gave into sin and killed his brother Abel and lived the consequences for the rest of his life. Unlike Cain, realize that as God said sin lies at the door, and it wants to destroy you and the life of your loved ones, but you should rule over it and can in victory through the Lord Jesus Christ.

ABOUT THE AUTHOR

Erika Grey, author, Bible scholar, commentator, journalist has been a born-again Christian for over 40 years She has written numerous books on Bible Prophecy and made contributions in helping to decode the more difficult forecasts. She has spoken on numerous radio stations including Coast to Coast.

This book is one of a series of short books by Erika Grey intended to be quick reads with important information. Be sure to check out Erika's other titles at www.erikagrey.com.

www.ingramcontent.com/pod-product-compliance
Lightning Source LLC
Chambersburg PA
CBHW050528170426
43201CB00013B/2133